Delightful

color by
numbers

Delightful
color by numbers

SIRIUS

SIRIUS

This edition published in 2021 by Sirius Publishing, a division of
Arturus Publishing Limited,
26/27 Bickels Yard, 151–153 Bermondsey Street,
London SE1 3HA

ISBN: 978-1-3988-1466-0
CH010171
Supplier 29, Date 1121, Print run 11934

Printed in China

Created for children 10+

INTRODUCTION

You'll discover that concentrating on coloring in one of these delightful images is one of the best ways to relax. Just the act of focusing on your artwork, and making sure you fill in the outlines with as much care and skill as you can, will push other worries out of the way for a pleasurable couple of hours or so.

And this book has a really wonderful selection of images for you to choose from. The gorgeous colors of a stunning Atlas moth, the vigor of a grizzly bear fishing for salmon in a free-flowing river, the splendor of a displaying peacock—as well as the glory of a marvelous sunset—are among the many images to enjoy here. There are also versions of famous sculptures such as 'The Thinker' and the Statue of Liberty. And for when you want a repeating pattern to focus on, there are tessellations and other patterns with plenty of lovely detail.

The handy size of this book allows you to take it with you wherever you go. So choose a peaceful spot, select the artwork that you want to color, follow the key at the back of this book, take your favorite pencils, and start to create your own special artwork. And chill while you do it.

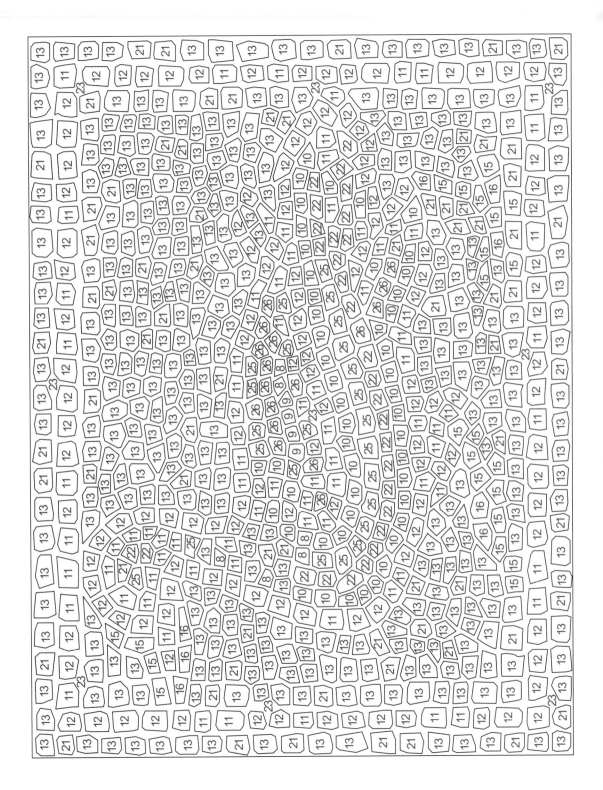

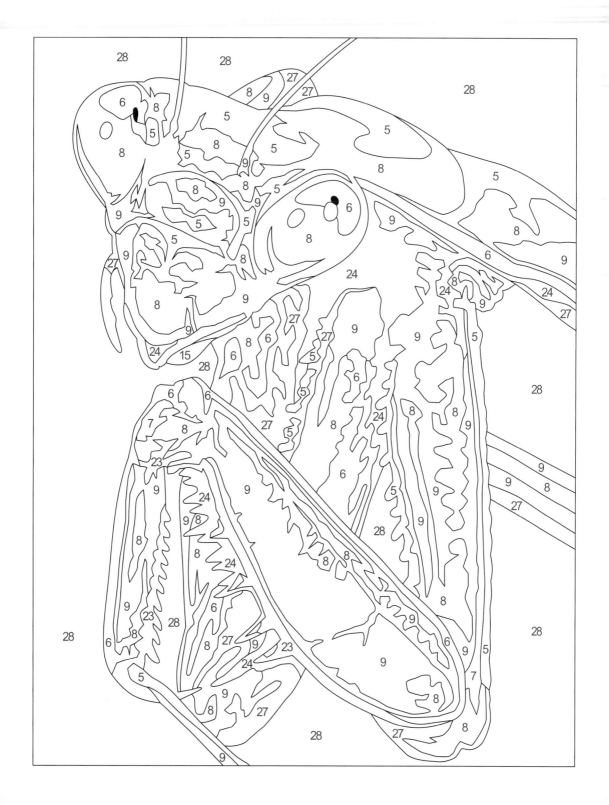

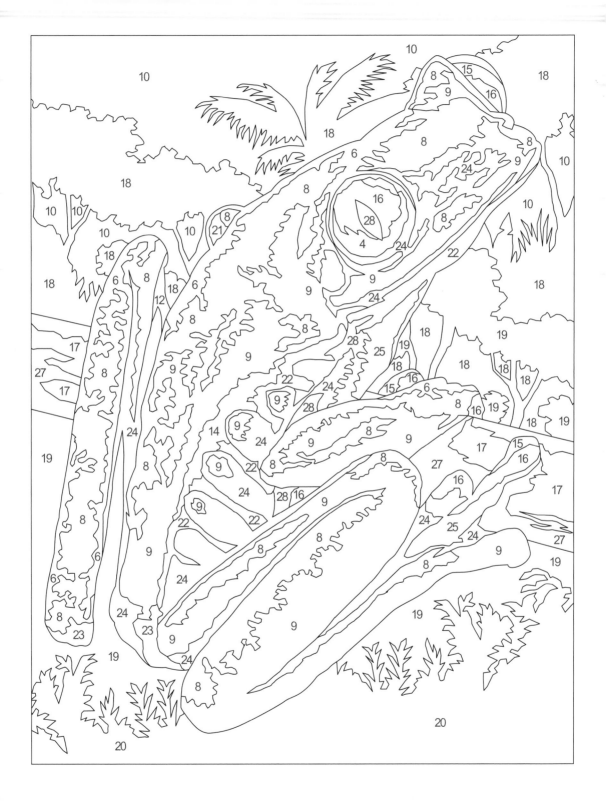

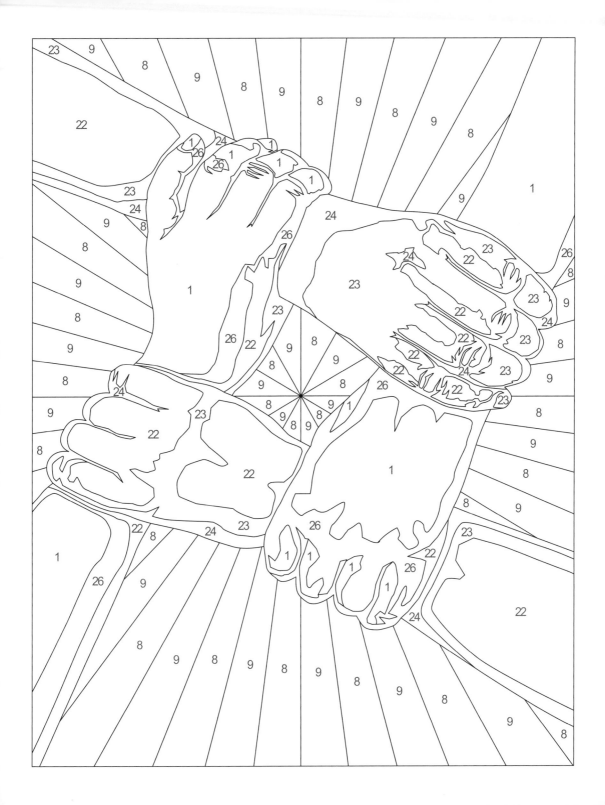

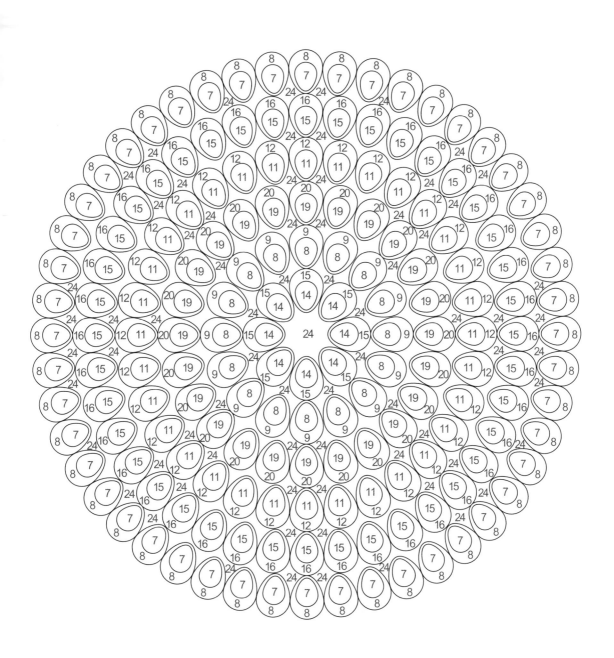